GIANT LANDSCAPES
Yorkshire Dales

A photographic journey around a unique area
of natural beauty

Dave Coates

MYRIAD BOOKS

Swaledale

Swaledale is the most northerly of the main dales. This dale is famous for its spring meadows and the wonderful array of field barns. The glacial action that formed the dale has left the farmers with areas of good bottom land, such as those at Gunnerside and Muker. Over the years, this land has been turned into patterns of fields bounded by the famous drystone walls, which now reach up the sides of the fells. There is an intimate quality about the dale because it is fairly narrow so the fellsides are never far away.

Barns and meadows of Gunnerside Bottoms (below)
Without any doubt one of the visitor's favourite places in Swaledale – and there are many – is Gunnerside Bottoms. This is a fertile stretch of old glacial flood plain that has been turned into a patchwork quilt of fields. Each field is bordered by drystone walls and many have their own traditional field barn. It is seen here at its best in evening light, in early June when the meadows are in full flower.

Storm clouds gathering over the meadows
Even on a spring morning the weather can change and give an oppressive feeling to the landscape. Here, in early morning in late May, the sun shines in from the east while threatening storm clouds gather from the west. The result is a landscape of beauty and drama.

Open stile leading through the meadows

A number of footpaths thread through this maze of fields and barns. Access to the fields is usually by means of simple gate stiles like this one. But watch out for the gate closing behind you – some of them have quite powerful return springs which have resulted in many a hapless walker getting a sharp rap on the ankles as the gate swings closed after them!

Oxnop Ghyll and its meadow land

Small tributary dales leading away from the main dales often have their own visual treats for the visitor who has time to wander off the beaten track. Oxnop Ghyll is no exception. Here the meadows fill the foreground, while the farmstead nestles in a dip under the lea of the fellside. The farm has been sited here not just for shelter but also to be near a source of running water from the stream behind.

Field patterns of Gunnerside

There often seems to be little reason for the random and crooked shapes of the fields. But what has resulted is a scene of real beauty – a wonderful example of how a combination of the landscape and livestock farming has created a scene of real beauty.

Gill Head towards Satron Side

This is the view from the road to Askrigg in Wensleydale as it winds up Oxnop Ghyll. The undulating and rolling fells of Swaledale are clearly visible. In the foreground, the farmstead with its fields stands on a high point but is sheltered by a stand of mature trees. In the middle distance is Satron Side and in the far distance the heather-covered moors are on the other side of Swaledale.

Heather moors with Calver Hill behind

After the meadows have been cut, the display of colour in the Dale moves upwards away from the fields as the heather carpets the fells in a purple haze. In the foreground are the moors near Surrender Bridge and Calver Hill is in the distance.

Oxnop Scar, towards Muker

If you take the gated and little used road along the eastern side of Oxnop Ghyll you will enjoy this magnificent view. On the right are the limestone crags of Oxnop Scar with the contrasting screes of shale below. The light and shade caused by passing clouds helps to emphasise features in the landscape. In the distance is Swaledale and beyond it Swinner Gill and the Kisdon Fells.

Muker with Kisdon Fell behind

The land around Muker in Swaledale can rival even the famous Gunnerside for the beauty of its spring meadows. This photograph is taken from Muker Side looking into the dale; the village of Muker lies to the left of the picture. The view is of a broad sweep of glorious spring meadows stretching out across the valley floor and up the lower slopes of the surrounding fells. The scattering of farmsteads and field barns complements the rest of the scene.

Upper Swaledale from Buttertubbs Pass

The dale has many moods and this photograph of the upper dale, taken from the Hawes to Thwaite road in winter, looks down and across a dale overshadowed by lowering skies. But even on the most cloudy of days, small breaks in the cloud allow the sun to light up the surrounding fells like a patchwork quilt.

Swaledale above Gunnerside

This photograph of Swaledale just above Gunnerside was taken on a lovely November morning. The full clarity of early light brings out the autumn colours and highlights the barns and farms dotted across the fellside.

Evening sunlight near Angram

In the hills above Thwaite, close to the little hamlet of Angram, sheep graze in the meadow as the shadow of the evening sun extends across them. The typical stone-built barn, with its faded red paintwork and the fellside beyond, provides a perfect counterpoint. Despite the beauty of the scene more practical thoughts often occur when you look at a scene such as this. How, for example, did the farmstead on the distant fell ever manage to provide anyone with a living?

Field barns near Thwaite

These field barns stand in the warm winter sun like sentries at the foot of the fellside. Simply constructed, the barns were very effective for the purpose for which they were built. The lower floor was usually a shelter for animals, normally sheep or cattle; the upper floor was used to store winter fodder.

East Gill

East Gill falls are located at the foot of East Stonesdale and close to the intersection of the two most famous long-distance walks in the north of England: the Pennine Way and the Coast to Coast walk. On its way to join the Swale in less than a couple of hundred yards, they carry East Gill over this lovely tiered limestone formation, producing a wonderful tumbling flow of water as it cascades downwards.

Wain Wath Falls

The area around Keld has a plethora of stunning waterfalls. The Wain Wath Falls are more familiar to most visitors because they are visible from the West Stonesdale road. The falls are made even more attractive by their dramatic setting beneath the rugged limestone crags of Cotterby Scar. In this picture, the patterns of foam that had formed into spectacular swirls after tumbling over the falls are particularly striking.

Morning light

Wain Wath Falls is really a line of several individual smaller falls all lined up along the same outcrop of rock. This picture, taken in the early morning light, takes advantage of this by concentrating on just three sections of the falls. The warm sunlit rocks in the foreground add a touch of contrast and depth to the rest of the scene.

Birkdale Beck and Whitsundale Beck
This junction of these two streams could rightly be called the source of the Swale, for it is at this point that Birkdale Beck flowing in from the right of the picture joins Whitsundale Beck and becomes the River Swale itself.

The infant Swale flows toward Keld
The infant River Swale is seen here winding its way down the dale and past Cotterby Scar under an early autumn sky. The grasses have all gone to seed, changing the summer green of the fields to yellow with the odd tree also beginning to turn in colour.

Birkdale and High Bridge
This picture serves as a reminder of how hard the climate in the high dales can be. With High Bridge in the foreground, the view takes you up into the far reaches of Birkdale right at the head of Swaledale. The fact that this picture was taken on a late spring bank holiday Monday, with snow still dusting the far fells, speaks volumes about the Yorkshire Dales.

Wensleydale

Wensleydale runs parallel to Swaledale just over the fell and to the south. But it is a dale of completely different character to its near neighbour since it is on a much larger scale. For most of its length, Wensleydale is the broadest of the Yorkshire Dales and is not as intimate as its partner to the north. Wander about Wensleydale, however, and you will find so much to enjoy, often tucked away in corners and in the tributary dales which are so common. Above all, the dale has a rich vein of waterfalls created by the waters of the River Ure and its tributaries, tumbling down over the limestone steps created by the Yoredale Series limestone. This dale is less remote and has a rich history – its abbeys and castles bear witness to this. But one thing Wensleydale does have in common with all of the Yorkshire Dales is its natural beauty, particularly its attractive meadow land, wild flowers and field barns.

Coverdale valley

Stretching away from the main dale near to Middleham is Coverdale, the first of many of Wensleydale's tributary dales. Coverdale quickly opens up into typical dales farmland with its meadows and barns set against a backdrop of less cultivated moorland. This scene is typical, with the cattle in the near meadow and the odd field ploughed up for cultivation. Beyond that are higher sheep meadows with fields surrounded by drystone walls and dotted with field barns.

Middleham Castle from the hill above

Middleham Castle, two miles south of Leyburn, was once the stronghold of the Warwick family and King Richard III during the Wars of the Roses. It stands defiantly against the ravages of time overlooking the lower part of Wensleydale. The buildings clustered at its base form part of the famous horse-racing stables of Middleham. They remind you of how many local homes would be clustered under the walls of the castle for protection in medieval times.

Castle Bolton

Castle Bolton stands proudly overlooking the dale. A loyalist stronghold in the civil war it was rendered almost indefensible by Cromwell after a prolonged siege. The building has been lovingly restored over recent years and is well worth a visit. Many rooms are still as they were when Mary Queen of Scots was imprisoned here. The re-planting of a medieval herb garden and maze add to the atmosphere of the castle.

Sheep and dales barn, early spring

In very early spring, the bracken on the fells still glows gold in the sunlight. This flock of expectant ewes is confined to the lower meadows for protection against the worst of the dales' weather and to be near to the shepherd as lambing time approaches. The scene must have remained essentially unchanged for centuries. The barn adds to this timeless quality, as the building would have been used for storing winter fodder before tractors were the norm in farming circles.

West Burton Falls

Wensleydale is a place of hidden nooks and crannies and Bishopdale is no exception. West Burton Falls are tucked away in a quiet little corner of the village of West Burton. Seen here on an October afternoon, Walden Beck appears almost graceful as it tumbles down out of the autumn woodland and into the little gladed pool. The dark still waters of the pool with the shimmering reflection of the trees only adds to the feeling of peace and beauty.

Autumn colours in Waldendale

Looking down the little dale of Waldendale and back into Bishopdale you can see that, in many places, its steep sides are wooded. In the late afternoon, just before the sun dips down behind the fell, the autumn colours of the trees are seen in all their glory. It is as if nature is trying to put on a last defiant show before the onset of winter.

Semer Water from the overlooking fells

Semer Water, a glacial lake, lies in a hanging valley left over by the ice age and surrounded by limestone fells. Seen here from one of the limestone crags, the skyline is dominated by the dramatic form of Addlebrough standing like a sentinel on the far side of the valley. In the distance beyond, the repetitive shape of Penhill is visible. The foreground fellside glows gold in the late spring with the dead grasses left over from the previous year.

Semer Water in winter

It is always fascinating to return to locations in differing seasons and on this occasion the contrast between spring and winter is stark but beautiful. The lake is frozen and the low sun shines off its surface creating patterns of its own. Clouds are racing over the fells, with the threat of more snow to come. Even the infant River Bain – at three miles in length, the shortest river in England – is still partly frozen over.

Thoralby village in winter

Bishopdale is a tributary valley more or less opposite Castle Bolton. Here, in the depths of winter, the landscape is covered with snow, revealing all the more graphically the drystone walls that border the fields of the dales. The scattering of trees stripped of their leaves stand even more starkly against the landscape with the little village of Thoralby nestling at the foot of the fell.

The Upper Falls in autumn
Aysgarth Falls is, without doubt, one of the "hot spots" of tourism in Wensleydale – and it is easy to see why. In the space of a couple of miles, the River Ure passes over a series of three major waterfalls created by the limestone landscape of the dale. The Upper Falls, pictured here in the autumn sunshine, provides a peaceful setting following a long dry summer. The autumn colours of the trees add to the apparent peace and beauty of the location.

Still waters of the Ure near Aysgarth
The river Ure flows peacefully less than a mile from the point at which it crashes over the famous Aysgarth Falls.

Middle falls in winter
Come back to Aysgarth Falls in a different season and the mood changes completely. In its winter colours, the landscape now takes on monochromatic tones with only the stone of the church and the slight peat staining in the water revealing that this is, in fact, a colour photograph.

Lower Falls in autumn

The Lower Falls are a closely-placed series of limestone ledges that combine to create the step-like nature of this waterfall. Like the neighbouring falls, the banks of the river are surrounded by trees. Here, in the autumn sunlight, the foliage helps to make a near perfect scene with the water making its way over each limestone ledge in graceful steps. Spreading away from the base of the falls is a whole series of smaller ridges over which the water then passes.

Hardraw Force

Hardaw Force is one of those "must visit" locations. The fall, which at 100ft (30m) is the highest free-falling waterfall in England, is at the head of a small gorge behind the village of Hardraw and is reached through the local Green Dragon Inn. If there is any sunlight, the spray from the crashing waters invariably creates a rainbow, especially around the middle of the day when the sun is at the correct angle.

Sunlit barn with Addlebrough

The contrast between this sunlit barn and meadow in the foreground and the distant sight of Addlebrough in shadow makes for a strikingly simple picture which catches the mood of a glorious dales evening. The blue-grey of the high clouds above only seems to add to this mood.

Hawes

The dale between Aysgarth and Hawes is a patchwork quilt of small communities, farmsteads, barns and drystone walls interspersed with trees scattered along the river bank or field margins. This view, in the evening light, across the dale to Hawes, is typical of the landscape of Wensleydale.

Hanging valley of Cotterdale

The moraine land left by the ice age means you actually climb up out of the main dale before entering the valley. Beyond the moraine is a small flood plain of good bottom land that supports the small farming community of the dale. Hidden away from casual view it remains a small, but very real, cameo of life in the dales.

Winter frosts

In winter the landscape changes in colour and mood. Instead of the greens and yellows of summer and autumn, the browns of dead vegetation dominate the scene. The path which leads into Cotterdale displays these seasonal changes.

Askrigg

Askrigg nestles into the northern flank of the dale. The town was once the main centre of the upper dale, since it lies close to the old Roman roads that lead either over Stake Pass to Ilkley or further west over Cam Fell. When the turnpike roads opened, trade and commerce went to Hawes instead. Askrigg achieved fame when it became the location for filming the television series *All Creatures Great and Small*, inspired by the Yorkshire vet James Herriot. Here the rooftops of the houses that line the narrow winding main street glisten in the winter light as the residents stoke up their fires against the cold.

Wharfedale

Wharfedale starts in the high fells and flows eastwards, as if to run parallel to and south of Wensleydale. However, the glacier that formed the dale came up against the huge mass of the fells of Buckden Pike and Great Whernside. This forced it to make a right turn and flow southwards so that Wharfedale now emerges to the south of the national park. Like Swaledale it is a narrow dale and has an intimate quality with the fells close by at all times. Wharfedale's landscape has been greatly affected by the Craven Fault, which thrust huge sections of great slab limestone to the surface and this is at its most spectacular at Kilnsey Crag.

Burnsall village

The well-loved village of Burnsall with its five-arched bridge is situated in the middle of the dale. It is almost at a crossroads between the gritstone that lies downstream and the limestone country above.

Bolton Priory in autumn light

We start our journey at Bolton Abbey – or Bolton Priory as it is more properly known. Viewed from the shelf of wooded hillside over the river, the autumn colours of the trees add a touch of magic to an already beautiful landscape. Located on a bend in the river the old abbey buildings occupy a prime position beside the River Wharfe. The abbey and its grounds, which extend for 30,000 acres across both sides of the dale, are owned and maintained by the Duke of Devonshire.

The Strid

Deep in the gorge is the feature that gives this area its name. The Strid – or stride – is little more than a crack in the rock bed of the gorge through which all the waters of the River Wharfe have to squeeze. It is a place where nature has produced dramatic beauty. But it is also a place that can lead the unwary to tragedy – the sides of the gorge are slippery and the force of the water while exhilarating is unforgiving.

River Wharfe and Strid Wood

In this photograph of Strid Wood the River Wharfe is emerging from the gorge, with the trees all around at their very best in autumn colour. The rapid-like waters of the river tumble in a mix of white and deep blue as they pass over the rock-strewn river bed.

Littondale from Arncliffe Cote

Littondale reaches into the high fells of the dales and the River Skirfare flows down it eventually joining the River Wharfe between Conistone Pie and Kilnsey Crag. The dale has its own distinct style of small villages separated by the usual patchwork quilt of fields bounded by drystone walls and scattered with field barns. Seen here from the side of Arncliffe Cote, on the old monk's road, the dale stretches out before you with the limestone crags and heather of Old Cote Moor.

Conistone limestone pavement

Make the effort to climb the crag above the Dales Way and you will discover this wonderful limestone pavement laid out before you with the occasional isolated tree dotted around. Limestone pavements were created during the Ice Age, when glaciers scraped the earth from the underlying limestone. Over the millennia, since the glaciers receded, the chemicals in snow and rainwater have worked away at the limestone to produce the wonderful pattern of "grikes" – gaps or fissures – in the surface of the pavement.

Conistone Pie

Conistone Pie is a picturesque feature, an isolated circular plinth of limestone which stands like a sentinel overlooking Wharfedale. The cairn on the top helps to enhance the name by which it is popularly known. That this solitary piece of limestone got left behind by the power of the glacier is almost unbelievable. Thankfully, like many other unusual features of the limestone dales, it is there for us to enjoy.

Cupola smelting works

The tributary valley of Hebden Gill winds away from the main valley and up into the hills behind Grasssington. The industrial past comes to life here in the form of the Cupola Smelting Works. A network of tunnels leads across the moors to chimneys like this one which has been carefully preserved. The idea was to let the gasses from the smelting process pass up the tunnels to cool and deposit the lead in them on the tunnel walls. Children were then sent along the tunnels to recover the precious metal.

The upper dale from Conistone Pie

Across the dale from Kilnsey is one of the best-loved spots in the dales. Under the lea of Conistone Pie is a glorious picnic place, located close to the Dales Way, from which there is a wonderful view of Upper Wharfedale. Old Cote Moor, on the left, gives way to Upper Wharfedale itself and, on the right, the mass of Buckden Pike rises above the eastern side of the dale.

Towards Starbotton from Goat Scar Crag

The view from Goat Scar Crag gives a panoramic view of the upper dale. It takes you all the way up to Buckden and beyond to Langstrothdale Chase. From this perspective, the whole of the glacial valley is laid out before you. Field barns, originally built to store fodder and give shelter to livestock, are dotted across the valley bottom with fields bounded by drystone walls.

Hubberholme church

The little church at Hubberholme has to be high on any list of places to visit in Wharfedale. This early English place of worship is seen here in late winter with its graveyard a carpet of snowdrops. Wander inside to appreciate the original architecture and one of the few minstrel's roods that remain in an English church. In complete contrast, but blending in with the building, are the modern oak pews each with a little carved mouse on them depicting their maker: the famous furniture-maker, "Mousey" Thompson of Kilburn.

Langstrothdale and Hubberholme from the old Roman Road

The old Roman road linking the settlements of Ilkley and Bainbridge climbs north out of Wharfedale from Buckden village. Seen from the Roman road above Buckden, in the early autumn sunshine, one can clearly see the parish church of Hubberholme nestling among the trees at the foot of Langstrothdale Chase. The chase and its principal village of Buckden both got their names during the period after the Norman invasion of Britain when this part of the dale was a deer-hunting estate. Nowadays, the chase and the village are a centre for tourism in the dale.

Langstrothdale in autumn

Langstrothdale is far more intimate than the larger dales. With the autumn colours falling more strongly on the fellsides than the trees, there is real beauty here. The wildness of the high fells is never far away yet, on a fine day like this with the water flowing gently by, you can be at peace with the world.

Upper Wharefdale

The River Wharfe in Langstrothdale is barely more than a small stream as it wends its way down the dale over a bed of limestone. The drystone walls on the far side are sufficiently set back to allow the route of the Dales Way to pass along the riverbank itself.

Malham and the Three Peaks

Towards the southern end of the Yorkshire Dales is one the most impressive features of its landscape, Malham Cove. It is perhaps the most magnificent manifestation the Craven Fault, the presence of which has done so much to create the unique landscape of the dales. We start here before moving across the moors to Upper Ribblesdale and around the Three Peaks of Pen-y-ghent (2,277ft/694m), Ingleborough (2,372ft/723m) and Whernside (2,415ft/ 736m). The limestone features and the results of glacial action really stand out; some the finest examples in Britain are to be found around Ingleborough and Crummackdale.

The outstanding geology of this area is due to the massive limestone slabs which were forced to the surface during the last ice age. Limestone is usually a dull, white colour since it is formed from the remains of millions of tiny sea-dwelling animals over the millennia. This helps to make it stand out dramatically among the dark colouring of the surrounding dales. The most impressive limestone features occur in crags such as Malham Cove or in large, flat areas called pavements. The pavements are worn down by the effects of wind and rain into "clints", or flat areas, and "grikes", which are fissures or gaps in the rock. Because limestone is easily eroded by chemicals in the air and water it is quickly weathered into unusual and dramatic shapes. Limestone is also porous, so surface water often disappears suddenly into sink holes such as those found above Malham.

Warrendale Knotts

The crags of Warrendale Knotts stand guard over the old green road below, well to the west of Malham Moor and on the fells overlooking Ribblesdale. They are more rounded than the cliffs of Malham or Kilnsey, with large amounts of loose stone screes.

Malham Cove

Before the permafrost thawed at the end of the last ice age, this massive 260ft (80m) limestone cliff was in all probability a gigantic waterfall. Today we have been left with one of the most dramatic features of the Yorkshire Dales limestone landscape, created by the Craven Fault which formed the limestone uplands.

Gordale Scar

Close to Malham Cove, Gordale Scar is an equally impressive sight. Created over thousands of years by vast torrents of water that poured down from the fell, we are now left with an awe-inspiring gorge with magnificent limestone crags and high overhanging fells. Water still tumbles down through a stone archway and waterfall at the head of the gorge. It is common for walkers to make their way up the side of the waterfall gradually climbing on to the moors beyond.

Pen-y-ghent from above the caves

Pen-y-ghent is also visible from the hills around Winskill. In the evening light of late summer the great bulk of the fell can be seen rising above the little farmsteads in Silverdale below. The course of a drystone wall can be traced climbing up the steep crags and over the summit itself. In times gone by, the boundaries of nearly all the parishes of the Dales were marked out by drystone walls.

Looking up Ribblesdale to Whernside

The great whale-shaped hump of Whernside at the head of Ribblesdale marks the skyline looking up the dale from the fellside above Horton in Ribblesdale. The combination of little limestone outcrops, drystone walls and barns is typical of this part of the dale. At the top of Ribblesdale is Ribblehead, famous for the Ribblehead Viaduct, where the Settle to Carlisle railway line crosses the moor.

Ingleborough from the Winskill Stones

Follow the track from Attermire and Warrendale Knotts northwards and you will eventually overlook Upper Ribblesdale near the Winskill Stones. Seen below in the foreground, they provide a striking counterpoint to this view across the dale towards Ingleborough, which is covered in snow on the distant skyline. The hamlet of Upper Winskill is in the middle distance and the scars from quarrying, near Helwith Bridge, are evident on the far fellside.

Ingleborough in low cloud

The early morning light and changeable weather often produce
atmospheric landscapes. Here, the sky is full of drama with the light
pouring through the clouds which are swirling around the summit of
Ingleborough. The fells in the middle distance are in deep shadow from
the clouds overhead, but are in complete contrast to the tranquil spring
scene with sheep and their lambs grazing contentedly in the foreground.

Limestone pavement above the dry valley

The waters that once poured over Malham Cove go underground at the
"water sinks" leaving a "dry valley" between them and Malham Cove.
The long lines of clints and grikes in this limestone pavement, which
overlooks the "dry valley", are displayed in a spectacular fashion in the
late afternoon light. In the distance, Dean Moor Hill (with the Pennine
Way making its way around its flanks) lies to the left and Combe Hill and
the Watlowes to the centre and right of the skyline.

Ravenscar and Ingleborough

Under the lea of the northern face on Ingleborough lies Ravenscar, a series
of limestone pavements that stretch out along a plateau of land under the
fell. A lonely thistle flowers defiantly from one of the grikes, surrounded
by the broad clints that are so typical of Ravenscar.

Twin Pecca Falls

The waterfalls in the two valleys which begin at Ingleton are some of
the finest in the dales. As you follow the course of the River Twiss, one
of the first waterfalls that you come to after crossing Pecca Bridge is the
Twin Pecca falls, pictured here. In a series of steps, the water tumbles
98ft (30m) over the rock formations surrounded by the high sides of the
valley which almost form a gorge around the river.

Dentdale from Deepdale

Take the road up Kingsdale from Ingleton and, once over the watershed,
you will discover this panoramic view down Deepdale and into
Dentdale. On the left of the picture the Howgill Fells can be seen in the
distance. On this fine late June day, the freshly cut meadows add a
variety of colours to a green and fertile landscape.

Drumlins near Ribblehead

The glorious late evening light shows off the undulating terrain at the head
of Ribblesdale to its best effect. Known as drumlins, these rolling lines of
hillocks are formed of boulder clay rocks and pebbles, and were created by
glacial action. The sunlight has picked out the gable ends of the barns and the
lines of drystone walls as they seem to wander over the rolling landscape.

Cottongrass *(Cyperaceae eriophorum)* and meadows

High on the fells at the head of Dentdale is this attractive view across wild
and uncultivated moorland. In the foreground is a mass of cottongrass, blowing
gently in the summer breeze. The contrast between the cultivated fields on the
distant fellside and the wild moorland landscape below is unusual.

Roadside flowers

At this time of year the road verges along the valley in Dentdale are covered in a rich variety of wild flowers. In this quiet lane with the old barn as a backdrop you will find common vetch, red campion, dog roses, meadow cranesbill and many more.

Dent Town

The village of Dent Town is the main centre and for many the chief attraction in Dentdale. It is a few miles south-east of the market town of Sedbergh. With its narrow but well-maintained cobbled streets lined with period buildings, this little gem is the quintessential place to stop and browse. Here the freshly whitewashed row of shops and cottages takes you back to a former age.

Crummackdale

Tucked away between Ribblesdale and Ingleborough is a little dale that epitomises all that is best about the limestone dales of Yorkshire. Crummackdale is not a big place – barely five miles long – but its small scale is more than compensated for by the views. From the fells around Crummackdale, you can enjoy some of the finest limestone scenery to be found anywhere. To enjoy it though, you will have to walk because roads are – thankfully perhaps – very scarce.

Limestone view to Pen-y-ghent

In this view, again with a glorious sky overhead, we can see across the head of the dale, with Moughton Scar in the middle distance and the great massive form of Pen-y-ghent standing proud on the skyline. It is difficult to believe that this landscape was created over 300 million years ago at the bottom of a tropical sea.

Limestone arch

This photograph of a limestone arch is taken from a low position to get a good view of its base. The plinth stone is perched so finely that you would not think it could withstand the power of the elements, especially in winter, but it does.

The lone tree

An impression of the vast panoramas to be seen on this route can be gained from this view of the upper reaches of the dale, which are bounded by the massive Moughton Scars. Taken from the western ridge this lone tree seems to emphasise the sheer grandeur of Crummackdale

The limestone pavement from Sulber Gate

At the head of the dale you come to Sulber Gate, from where you can look down on the almost unbelievable view of what is one of the most sensational of all the limestone pavements in the Yorkshire Dales. Literally stretching for miles, the pavement continues right on to the top of Moughton Fell itself. To the right, Crummackdale leads away southwards and, in the distance, some 20 miles away and well into Lancashire, is the unmistakeable shape of Pendle Hill.

Evening sky over Moughton

Between Moughton Scar and Moughton Fell you come to an old packhorse route which leads you back down into the dale, across limestone meadows and eventually back to your starting point. This photograph, taken from the track, shows the mass of Moughton Fell combined with the lonely tree and a wonderful evening sky. Crummackdale is a place which draws visitors back time and time again. It is the essence of what the limestone dales are about on a grand but also intimate scale.

First published in 2004 by Myriad Books Limited
35 Bishopsthorpe Road, London SE26 4PA

Photographs and text copyright © Dave Coates

Dave Coates has asserted his right under the Copyright, Designs and
Patents Act, 1988, to be identified as the author of this work

ISBN 1 904736 17 3

Designed by Jerry Goldie

Printed in China